Athletics

The Complete Overview

Dilbir Singh
B.P.E., B.P.Ed., M.P.Ed., UGC (SET)
Physical Education Teacher,
Dept. of Youth Services and Sports,
Govt. of Jammu and Kashmir
&
Pawan Kumar
M.P.Ed., M.Phil., UGC NET/SET
Physical Education Teacher, Dept. of Youth Services and Sports, Govt. of Jammu and Kashmir

KSK
KHEL SAHITYA KENDRA
7/26, Ansari Road, Daryaganj,
New Delhi-110002

Published by:

KHEL SAHITYA KENDRA

7/26, Ansari Road, Darya Ganj, New Delhi-110002

Ph.: (O) 011-43551324, 42564726, 47090343
(M) 9811088729, (Fax) 011-42564726
(Res.) 47091605

E-mail: khelsahitya1@rediffmail.com

Website: www.khelsahitya.com, www.kskpublisher.com

ISBN 978-81-946581-0-8

PRINTED IN INDIA 2022

Printed by:
ASIAN OFFSET PRINTERS
Delhi

Laser Typesetting by:
K.S.K. DTP UNIT, DELHI

ATHLETICS

(A COMPLETE OVERVIEW)

Dilbir Singh
B.P.E., B. P. Ed, M. P. Ed. , UGC (SET)
Physical Education Teacher, Dept. of Youth Services and Sports, Govt. of Jammu and Kashmir

Pawan Kumar
M. P. Ed. , M. Phil., UGC NET, UGC SET
Physical Education Teacher, Dept. of Youth Services and Sports, Govt. of Jammu and Kashmir

DEDICATED

TO

MY FATHER

PREFACE

The book has been especially prepared for the new students of physical education along with this, the people who are not associated with Athletics and want to know about Athletics, they can easily attain the fundamental knowledge about the "Types of Events ", "Number of Events" and some basic rules associated with the different events of Track and Field. This book is specially designed for the people who are eager to have the basic knowledge about athletics. It will be proved valuable to those who are beginners in athletics. In the last portion of this book, some scientific laws have been mentioned which knowingly and unknowingly effect the performance of a contestant. The text is divided into different sections; Rules of different events, way of execution of events, Throughout all the sections of the book an effort has been made to explain the basic concepts of marking in track and field in the easiest manner through examples. The book has been written in a simple language.

The book is designed especially for the beginners of athletics, who face difficulties while going through with the events of Athletics. This book is intended for the use as a text for undergraduate as well as post graduate students of physical education. This text would cater the need of under graduate and post graduate students in physical education of all Indian colleges and universities. The goal of the text is to provide the students with competence in the basic concepts of athletics in physical education. Most of the reasoning relating to track and field marking tried to be clarified in an easy way and in a simple language. In the rules section latest rules of IAAF are discussed in a simple way for easy understanding of physical education students.

I hope that the book will prove its worth by fulfilling the needs of those for whom it has been specifically designed. Any suggestion for its improvement will be gratefully acknowledged and warmly appreciated.

I express my deep sense of gratitude to Dr. OMji Gupta, Assistant Professor, Physical Education and Associate NCC Officer Chhattisgarh Higher Education Department, who wrote a foreword to this book and also contributed directly or indirectly in the pursuit of completing this book, his suggestions and ideas were well taken and helped a lot.

I also express my gratitude to the most respected person in my life, Professor Uttam Chand Thakur, who helped me a lot, all the times when I felt difficulties in understanding things associated with Athletics.

I am indebted to many of my professional colleagues for encouraging me to write this book by providing some or the other concepts in physical education.

Finally, the personal support of my family during this project was invaluable. I express my appreciation to my mother for constant encouragement throughout this assignment. I acknowledge the efforts of my brother and sister and their families for supporting me morally and spiritually. Lastly, I appreciate the efforts of the children of my family, Sakshi, Varun and Suryansh who always keep me happy and energetic.

DILBIR SINGH

dsmanhas_123@yahoo.com

FOREWORD

It is a matter of great pleasure to write a foreword to the book titled "Athletics (a complete overview)" written by Mr. Dilbir Singh and Mr. Pawan Kumar (co-author). The book has been written in a simple language. The book has been especially prepared for the new students of physical education along with this, the people who are not associated with Athletics and want to know about Athletics. They can easily attain the fundamental knowledge about the "Types of Events ", "Number of Events" and some basic rules associated with the different events of Track and Field. This book is specially designed for the people who are eager to have the basic knowledge about athletics. It will be proved valuable to those who are beginners in athletics.

I congratulate Mr. Dilbir Singh and Mr. Pawan Kumar for their voluminous and incredible work. The book is recommended for School and College libraries.

Dr. OMji Gupta,
Assistant Professor Physical Education and Associate NCC Officer Chhattisgarh Higher Education Department.
(Chhattisgarh PSC Topper)

List of Contents

INTRODUCTION

Based on man's natural activities of running, jumping and throwing athletics is the oldest sport recorded in the history of human civilization. As organized sport extravaganza, the ancient Greeks gifted then to the modern world .Along with gymnastics and swimming, athletics is considered as a mother sport, the basis of all skill based of all skill based games and sport played these days. In American terminology athletics assumes a very wide meaning covering all sporting activity. Whether recreational or competitive, in technical sense of the term its usage is confined to track and field events, marathon road race and walking events. Athletics refers to track and field sports such as running, the high jump, and the javelin. Athletics refers to any kind of physical sports, exercise, or games. [US] students who play intercollegiate athletics. Track and field events have evolved over the thousands of years since the Greeks invented athletics with the first Olympics.

HISTORY OF ATHLETICS

The word "athletics" as it is internationally known sprang from university sport events in England in the 19th century. Through the origin of athletics is last in antiquity, it is quite certain that physical activity has been a part of the life of even primitive man. For him it might have been a basic necessity of life, more than fun and diversion for his survival depended on it Hunting, Fishing hurling missiles were activities on which his survival depended. Gradually along with the process of evolution, such activities became more of play and became part of the culture of the tribes people used these athletics event as a mode of transmitting the cultural heritage of their tribes. Today, these events have emerged as universal cultural phenomena. A Greek vase from 500BC depicting a running contest. The sport of track and field has its roots in human prehistory. Track and field-style events are among the oldest of all sporting competitions, as running, jumping and throwing are natural and universal forms of human physical expression. The first recorded examples of organized track and field events at a sports festival are the Ancient Olympic Games. At the first Games in 776 BC in Olympia, Greece, only one event was contested: the stadion footrace.[1] The scope of the Games expanded in later years to include further running competitions, but the introduction of the Ancient Olympic pentathlon marked a step towards track and field as it is recognised today – it comprised a five-event competition of the long jump, javelin throw, discus throw, the stadion foot race, and wrestling.

Track and field events were also present at the Panhellenic Games in Greece around this period, and they spread to Rome in Italy around 200 BC. After the period of Classical antiquity (in which the sport was largely Greco-Roman influenced) new track and field events began developing in parts of Northern Europe in the Middle Ages. The stone put and weight throw competitions popular among Celtic societies in Ireland and Scotland were precursors to the modern shot put and hammer throw events. One of the last track and field events to develop was the pole vault, which stemmed from competitions such as the Fierljeppen contests in the Northern European Lowlands in the 18th century.

Discrete modern track and field competitions, separate from general sporting festivals, were first recorded in the late 19th century. These were typically organised by educational institutions, military organisations and sports clubs as competitions between rival establishments. Competitive hurdling first came into being around this point, with the advent of the steeplechase in England around 1850. The Amateur Athletic Association was established in England in 1880 as the first national body for the sport of athletics and, under this grouping, track and field became the focus of the annual AAA Championships. The United States also began holding an annual national competition – the USA Outdoor Track and Field Championships – first held in 1876 by the New York Athletic Club. Following the establishment of general sports governing bodies for the United States (the Amateur Athletic Union in 1888) and France (the Union des sociétésfrançaises de sports athlétiques in 1889), track and field events began to be promoted and codified.

The establishment of the modern Olympic Games at the end of the 19th century marked a new high for track and field. The Olympic athletics programme, comprising track and field events plus a marathon race, contained many of the foremost sporting competitions of the 1896 Summer Olympics. The Olympics also consolidated the use of metric measurements in international track and field events, both for race distances and for measuring jumps and throws. The Olympic athletics programme greatly expanded over the next decades, and track and field contests remained among the Games' most prominent. The Olympics was the elite competition for track and field, and only amateur sportsmen could compete. Track and field would continue to be a largely amateur sport, as this rule was strictly enforced: Jim Thorpe was stripped of his track and field medals from the 1912 Olympics after it was revealed that he had played baseball professionally.

That same year, the International Amateur Athletic Federation (IAAF) was established, becoming the international governing body for track and field, and it enshrined amateurism as one of its founding principles for the sport. The National Collegiate Athletic Association held their first Men's Outdoor Track and Field Championship in 1921, making it one of the most prestigious competitions for students, and this was soon followed by the introduction of track and field at the inaugural World Student Games in 1923. The first continental track and field competition was the 1919 South American Championships, which was followed by the European Athletics Championships in 1934. Up until the early 1920s, track and field had been almost exclusively a male-only pursuit. The women's sports movement led to the introduction of five track and field events for women in the athletics at the 1928 Summer Olympics and more women's events were gradually introduced as years progressed (although it was only towards the end of the century that the men's and women's programmes approached parity of events). Furthermore, major track and field competitions for disabled athletes were first introduced at the 1960 Summer Paralympics.

With the rise of numerous regional championships, as well as the growth in Olympic-style multi-sport events (such as the Commonwealth Games and the Pan-American Games), competitions between international track and field athletes became widespread. From the 1960s onwards, the sport gained more exposure and commercial appeal through television coverage and the increasing wealth of nations. After over half a century of amateurism, the amateur status of the sport began to be displaced by growing professionalism in the late 1970s. As a result, the Amateur Athletic Union was dissolved in the United States and it was replaced with a non-amateur body solely focused on the sport of athletics: The Athletics Congress (later USA Track and Field). The IAAF soon followed suit in 1982, abandoning amateurism, and later removing all references to it from its name by rebranding itself as the International Association of Athletics Federations. The following year saw the establishment of the IAAF World Championships in Athletics – the first ever global competition for just athletics which became one of track and field's most prestigious competitions along with the Olympics.

The profile of the sport reached a new high in the 1980s, with a number of athletes becoming household names (such as Carl Lewis, Sergey Bubka, Sebastian Coe, Zola Budd and Florence Griffith-Joyner). Many world records were broken in this period, and the added political element between competitors of the United States, East Germany, and the Soviet Union, in reaction to the Cold War, only served to stoke the sport's popularity. The increase in the commercial capacity of track and field was also met with developments in the application of sports science, and there were many changes to coaching methods, athlete's diet regimes, training facilities and sports equipment. This was also accompanied by an increase in the use of performance-enhancing drugs, and prominent cases, such as those of Olympic gold medalists Ben Johnson and Marion Jones, damaged the public image and marketability of the sport.

From the 1990s onwards, track and field became increasingly more professional and international, as the IAAF gained over two hundred member nations. The IAAF World Championships in Athletics became a fully professional competition with the introduction of prize money in 1997, and in 1998 the IAAF Golden League — an annual series of major track and field meetings in Europe — provided a higher level of economic incentive in the form of a US$1 million jackpot. In 2010, the series was replaced by the more lucrative IAAF Diamond League which comprises meetings in Europe, Asia, North America and the Middle East – the first ever worldwide annual series of track and field meetings.

CLASSIFICATION OF ATHLETICS

Athletics are classified into track and field events. Track events are further categorized into Sprint race (100m, 200m, 400m, 400m hurdler and 110m hurdles for men and 100m hurdlers for women) Middle distance races (800m, 1500m) and Distance races (3000m, 5000m,) Marathon , cross country, steeple chase, relay races and walking events also fall under this category. Field events constitute jumping events (high jump, running broad jump, pole vault, triple jump) and throwing events (discus, javelin, shot and hummer)

GENDER AND AGE WISE LIST OF EVENTS

MEN AND JUNIOR MEN UNDER 18 & 19 YEARS		WOMEN AND JUNIOR UNDER 18 & 19 YEARS	
1.	100m	1.	100m
2.	200m	2.	200m
3.	400m	3.	400m
4.	800m	4.	800m
5.	1500m	5.	1500m
6.	5000m	6.	3000m
7.	10000 M	7.	10000m
8.	110m Hurdler(106.7cm)	8.	100m Hurdler(84.0cm)
9.	400m Hurdler(91.4 cm)	9.	400m hurdler(76.2cm)
10.	3000m steeple chase	10.	Long jump
11.	Long jump	11.	High jump
12.	High jump	12.	Triple jump
13.	Triple jump	13.	Pole vault
14.	Pole vault	14.	Shot put (4Kg)

15.	Shot put (7.260 Kg)	**15.**	Discus (1Kg)
16.	Discus (2 Kg)	**16.**	Javelin (600 gm)
17.	Javelin (800 gm)	**17.**	Hammer
18.	Hammer (7.260 Kg)	**18.**	4x100m Relay
19.	4x100m Relay	**19.**	4x400m Relay
20.	4x400m Relay	**20.**	Heptathlon
21.	Decathlon	**21.**	Walk (10Km)
22.	Walk (20/50 Km)	**22.**	Cross country
23.	Cross country (12Km)	**23.**	Marathon
24.	Marathon	24	Decathlon

NOTE: The Decathlon Event was not included in the list of events for women, but along with the passage of the time it has been initiated for women as well.

COMBINED EVENTS

MEN:

Pentathlon: Five events to be held on one day.

(Long jump, Javelin, 200m, Discus and 1500m)

Decathlon: (For men and Women both)

Ten events to be held on two consecutive days.

First day: 100m, Long jump, Shot put, High jump and 400m.

Second day: 110m Hurdles, Discus, Pole vault, Javelin and 1500m

WOMEN:

Heptathlon: Seven events to be held on two consecutive days.

First day: 100m Hurdles, High jump, Shot-put, and 200m.

Second day: Long jump, Javelin, & 800m

Decathlon: Ten events to be held on two consecutive days.

First day: 100m, Discus, Pole vault, Javelin and 400m.

Second day: 100m Hurdle, Long jump, Short put, High jump and 1500m.

Age wise number of Events: (For both men and women)

BOYS:

Below 20 years		**Below 18 years**		**Below 16 years**	
1.	100m	**1.**	100m	**1.**	100m
2.	200m	**2.**	200m	**2.**	400m
3.	400m	**3.**	400m	**3.**	800m
4.	800m	**4.**	800m	**4.**	3000m
5.	1500m	**5.**	1500m	**5.**	100m Hurdles(91.4cm)
6.	5000m	**6.**	5000m	**6.**	Long Jump
7.	10000m	**7.**	2000m steeple chase	**7.**	High Jump
8.	3000m steeple chase	**8.**	110m Hurdles (99.0cm)	**8.**	Shot Put (5Kg)

9.	110m Hurdle (106.7cm)	**9.**	Long jump	**9.**	Discus (1Kg)
10.	400m Hurdle (91.4cm)	**10.**	High jump	**10.**	Javelin (600gm)
11.	Long jump	**11.**	Triple jump	**11.**	4x100m Relay
12.	High jump	**12.**	Pole vault	**12.**	Pentathlon
13.	Triple jump	**13.**	Shot put (6Kg)	**13.**	Walk (5Km)
14.	Pole vault	**14.**	Discus (1.5Kg)		
15.	Shot put (7.26Kg)	**15.**	Javelin (800gm)		
16.	Discus (2Kg)	**16.**	Hammer (6Kg)		
17.	Javelin (800gm)	**17.**	4x100m Relay		
18.	Hammer (8.260 Kg)	**18.**	4x400m Relay		
19.	4x100m Relay	**19.**	Heptathlon		
20.	4x400m Relay	**20.**	Walk (10Km)		
21.	Decathlon				
22.	Walk (10Km)				

GIRLS:

Below 20 years		**Below 18 years**		**Below 16 years**	
1.	100m	**1.**	100m	**1.**	100m
2.	200m	**2.**	200m	**2.**	400m
3.	400m	**3.**	400m	**3.**	800m
4.	800m	**4.**	800m	**4.**	3000m
5.	1500m	**5.**	1500m	**5.**	100m Hurdles(83.8cm)
6.	3000m	**6.**	3000m	**6.**	Long Jump
7.	5000m	**7.**	110m Hurdle (83.8cm)	**7.**	High Jump
8.	110m Hurdle (83.8cm)	**8.**	Long jump	**8.**	Shot Put (4Kg)
9.	400m Hurdle (76.2cm)	**9.**	High jump	**9.**	Discus (1Kg)
10.	Long jump	**10.**	Triple jump	**10.**	Javelin (600gm)
11.	High jump	**11.**	Shot put (4Kg)	**11.**	4x100m Relay
12.	Triple jump	**12.**	Discus (1Kg)	**12.**	Pentathlon
13.	Shot put (4Kg)	**13.**	Javelin (600gm)	**13.**	Walk (3Km)

14.	Discus (1Kg)	**14.**	Hammer (4Kg
15.	Javelin (600gm)	**15.**	4x100m Relay
16.	Hammer (4Kg)	**16.**	4x400m Relay
17.	4x100m Relay	**17.**	Heptathlon
18.	4x400m Relay	**18.**	Walk (5Km)
19.	Heptathlon		
20.	Walk (5Km)		

COMBINED EVENTS FOR YOUTH

BOYS:

Octathalon: Eight events to be held on two consecutive days.

First day: 100m, Long jump, Shot put and 400m.

Second day: 110m Hurdle, high jump and 1000m

GIRLS:

Heptathlon: Seven events to be held on two days.

First day: 100m Hurdle, High jump, Shot put and 200m.

Second day: Long jump, Javelin and 800m.

BASIC REQUIREMENTS OF ATHLETICS

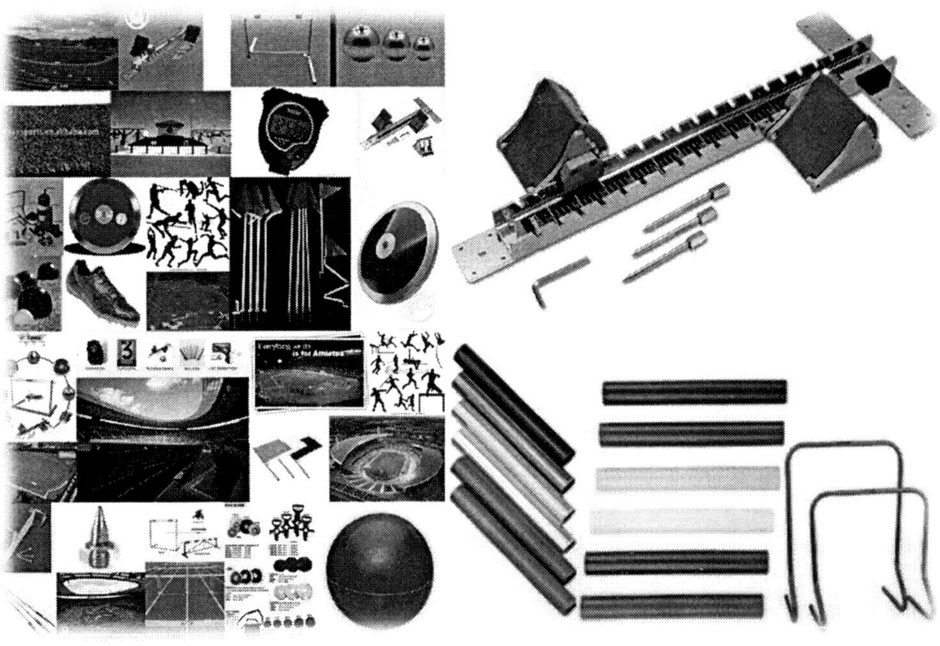

ATHLETIC TRACK

A Standard athletic track has length of 400m length 8 lanes. It shall consist of two parallel straight and two bends whose radius shall be equal sector for various throws and pit for jump are marked inside the field. Sometime jumping areas for long jump and pole vault are set outside the track to avoid crowding of events.

- While marking a standing track a few important points to remember are:-In all race up to and including 400m each athlete shall have a separate lane with a width of 1.22m to be marked by line 5cm in width.
- In all races up to and including 400m (including the first leg of the 4X200cm and 4X100m and 4X400m) the athletes shall use starting blocks.
- The width of the track should not be less than 7.32m (i.e. 6 lanes each lane being 1.22m width.

- Unless it is a grassy track the inner line of the track should have raised borders which can be made of concrete or any such material the approximate height and minimum width of the should necessarily be 5cm.

- When measuring the distance in track lanes 30cm should be left from the kerbs and in case there is no kerb 20cm should be left out in each lane.

- Except for first lane where the running distance is exactly 400m, in all other lanes a mathematically calculation stagger (an allowance of distance) is to be provided to compensate the excess distance that get increased due to the increase in radius as we wave out ware in each lane.

THE FULL STAGGERS AND HALF STAGGERS FOR EACH LANE ARE GIVEN BELOW

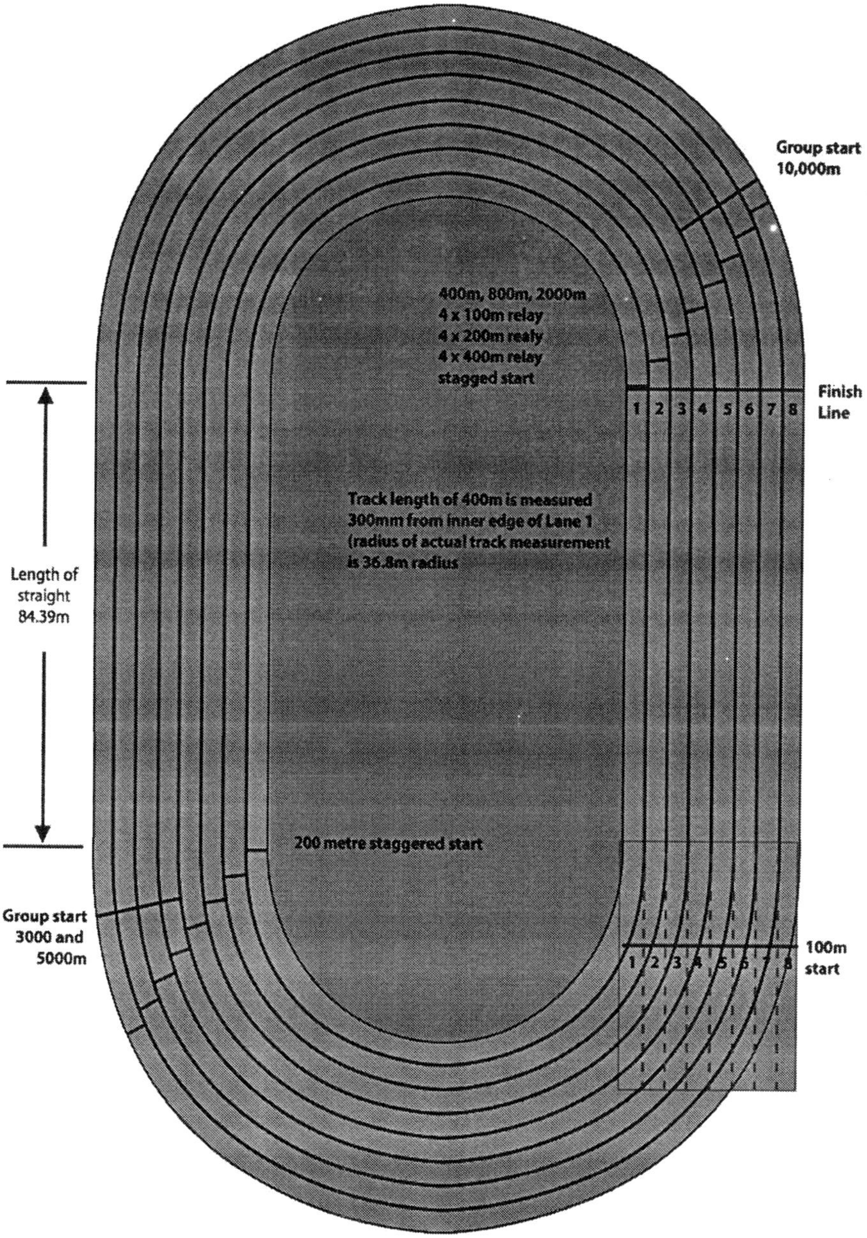

LANE	FULL STAGGER	HALF STAGGER
First	Nil	Nil
Second	07.04m	03.52m
Third	14.71m	07.35m
Fourth	22.38m	11.19m
Fifth	30.05m	15.02m
Sixth	37.72m	18.86m
Seventh	45.39m	22.69m
Eight	53.05m	26.52m

TRACK AND FIELD OFFICIALS

Management Officials:-

- One Competition Director.
- One Meeting Manager.
- One Technical Manager.
- One Call Room Manager.

Competition Officials:

- One or more Referee for Track Events.
- One or more Referee for Field Events.
- One or more Referee for Combined Events.
- One Referee for events outside the stadium.
- One Chief Judge adequate number of judges for Track Events.
- One Chief Judge and adequate number of judges for Field Events.
- One Chief Judge and eight Judges for each Track Race walking events; other Race Walking Competition officials (including recorders).
- One Chief umpires for Track Events.
- One Chief time keeper and an adequate number of Time keepers.
- One or more Starter.
- One or more Recalled.

- One or more Starter's Assistance.
- One or more Lap scorer.
- One or more Recorder.
- One or more Marshal.
- One or more wind gauge Operator.
- One or more Chief Photo-Finish Judge. Two assistant Photo-Finish Judges.
- One or more Measurement Judge (Electronics).
- One or more Call room Judge.

Additional Officials:

- One or more Announcer.
- One or more Statistician.
- One Advertising Commissioner.
- One Official Surveyor.
- One or more Doctor.
- Stewards for Competitions, Officials and Press.
- Referees and judges should wear a distinct armband or badge.

RUNNER RACES / WALKING EVENTS

1. Every athlete shall wear a distinct mark a number on his chest and back. Without a number he will not be allowed to participate.

2. An athlete can participate in an event bare-footed or with footwear. However, the footwear should not give him additional advantage of any in his performance.

3. All races shall be started by the actual report of a pistol or any similar apparatus upwards in the air but not before all the competitors are quite still on your marks.

4. At all international meets, the words of starter in his own mother tongue, shall be "on your marks", "set", and when all competitors are set, the pistol shall be fired.

5. If a competitor leaves his mark with hand or foot after the word set but before the shot is fired, it shall be considered a false start , this unfair start

and is also called "Beating the pistol" for this the athlete must be in contact with the track persists in it he may be disqualified.

6. Starting blocks or foot supports may be used, If they are used both feet of the athlete must be contact with the track while starting. Competitors may use their own starting blocks or foot supports.

7. Any competing runner or walker who jostles or obstructs another competitor so as to impede his progress, shall be liable to disqualification from that event. If in any race a competitor is disqualified of any race a competitor is disqualified for any of these reasons, the referee shall have the authority to order the to be re-held excluding the disqualified competitor or in the case of a heat to permit any competitor affected by the act resulting in disqualification to complete in a subsequent round of the race.

8. In all races run in lanes, each competitor shall keep within his allocated lane from start to finish. This shall also apply to any portion of a race run in lanes i.e. start of 800M.

9. If a competitor is punished or forced by another person to run outside his lane and if no material advantage is gained the competitor should not be disqualified

   If an athlete either.

   i. Runs outside his lane in the straight and no material advantage is gained or

ii. Runs outside the outer line of his lane on the bend with no material advantage thereby being gained the runner is not obstructed. Then he should likewise not be disqualified.

10. Apart from the above exceptions, if the referee is satisfied, on the report of or judge or umpire or otherwise that a competitor has rub outside his lane, he shall be disqualified.

11. An athlete, leaving the track voluntarily, shall not be allowed to compete in the race.

12. The finish of a race shall be denoted by a white line 5cm wide.

13. The athletes shall be placed in order in which any part of their bodies (i.e. torso, as distinguished from the head, neck, arms, legs, hands or feet) reaches the vertical plane of nearest edge of the finish line.

14. The time shall be taken from the flash/ smoke of the gun or approved starting apparatus to the moment at which any part of the body of an athlete i.e. torso reaches the perpendicular edge of the finish line.

15. Three official time- keepers (including the chief time-keeper) independently shall time the winner of ever event.

16. Preliminary rounds (heats) shall be held in track event in which the number of athletes is too large to allow satisfactory competition and a single round (final). Where preliminary rounds are held, all athletes must compete in and qualify through all such round (heats, quarter finals & semifinals).

17. The following minimum time must be allowed, when practicable, between the last heat of any round and the first heat of subsequent round or final.

- Up to including 200m 45 minutes
- Over 200m up to and including 1000m 90 minutes
- Over 1000m not on the same day.

HURDLES RACES

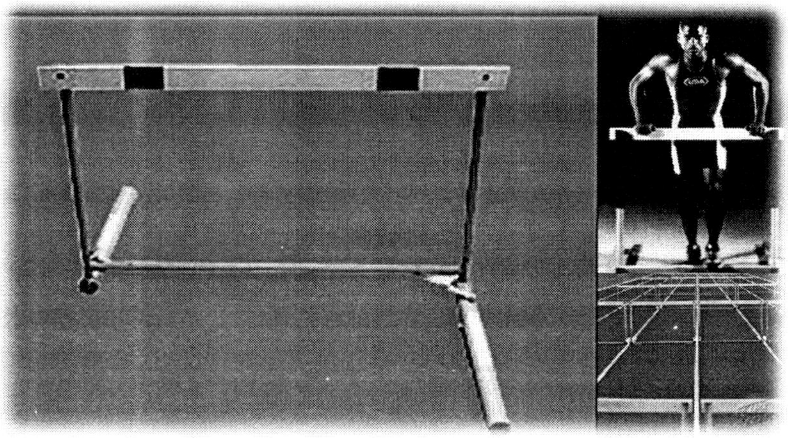

1. The following are the standard distance hurdle races for the two genders:

   - Men: 110m, 400m
   - Women: 100m, 400m

2. There shall be 10 hurdles in each lane, set out in accordance with the following table:

Gender	**Distance of Race**	**Distance from start line to first hurdle**	**Distance between Hurdles**	**Distance from last line hurdle to finish line**
Men, Junior Men and Youth	110m 400m	13.72 45.00	09.14m 35.00m	14.02m 40.00m

Boys				
Women ,Junior Women and Youth Girls	100m 400m	13.72 45.00	08.50m 35.00m	10.50m 40.00m

Each hurdle shall be so placed on the track that its feet shall be on the side of the approach by the competitor.

3. The standard height of the hurdles for different categories of athletes shall be:

Category of Athlete	**Distance of Race**	**Height of the hurdle**
1. Men/Junior Men	110m 400m	1.067m 0.914m
2. Youth Boys	110m 400m	0.914m 0.840m
3. Women/Junior Women	100m 400m	0.840m 0.762m
4. Youth Girl	100m 400m	0.762m 0.762m

Maximum width of the hurdle =1.18-1.20m. Maximum length of the base = 70cm. Total weight of the hurdle = not less than10Kg.

In each case there shall be a tolerance allowance of 3mm above and below the standard height, to allow for variation of the manufacture of the hurdles.

4. All races shall be run in lanes and each competitor shall keep to his own lane throughout.

5. A competitor who trails his foot or leg alongside any hurdle or jumps any hurdle not his own lane or deliberately knocks down any hurdle by hand shall be disqualified.

6. Except as provided in paragraph 5 above, the knocking down of hurdles shall not disqualify nor prevent a record being made.

STEEPLE CHASE RACES

1. The standard distances shall be 2000m (with 18 hurdle jumps and 5 water jumps) and 3000m (with 28 hurdle jumps and 7 water jumps)

2. The hurdle shall be 91.3cm high for men's events and 76.2cm for women's events, and shall be at least 3.96m wide. The section of the bar of the hurdles, and the hurdle at the water jump shall be 12.7cm square. The water jump, including the hurdle, shall be 3.66m in length and the water pit shall be 3.66m in width.

3. Each athlete shall go over or over or through the water and anyone who steps to the one side or other of the jump or trails his foot or leg below the horizontal plane of the any hurdle at the time of clearance shall be disqualified.

RELAY RACES

1. Chalk lines 50mm wide shall be drawn the track to mark the distances of the stages and to denote the scratch line.

2. Chalk lines 50mm wide shall also be drawn 10m before and after the scratch line to denote the take-over zone within which lines the baton must be exchanged. These lines are be include in the zone measurement.

3. In all relay races the baton must be passed within the take-over zone.

4. When a relay race is being run in lanes, a competitor may place one check-mark on the track within his own lane by using self-adhesive tape, maximum 5cm x 40cm, of distinctive colour which cannot be confused with other permanent markings. For a cinder or grass track, he may make a checkmark within his own line by scratching the track with his own shoe but may not place marking objects on or alongside the track.

5. The relay baton is a one piece smooth, circular hollow tube made of wood or metal or any rigid material, 28-30 cm in length and 12-13 cm in circumference, and weighs less than 50 gm. It shall be carried in hand throughout the races. If

dropped, the athlete who dropped it shall recover it. He may leave the lane to retrieve the baton provided that, by doing so, he does not lessen the distance to be covered. Provided that if this procedure is adopted, no other athlete is impeded, dropping the baton shall not result in disqualification. In all races, the baton shall be passed within the take-over zone. The passing of the baton commences when it is first touched by receiving runner and is completed the moment it is the hand of the receiving runner only. Within the take-over zone, it is only the position of the baton, which is decisive, and not the position of the body or limbs of the competitor.

6. The position of the teams at the start of the race shall be drawn, and shall be retained at each take over zone, except that the waiting runner can move to the inside position on the track as in-coming team mates arrive, provided that this can be done without fouling.

7. In events where the first part of race is to be run in lanes, the competitors, after completing this part, are free to take up any position on the track.

8. After handing over the baton, competitors should remain in their own lanes or zones until the course is clear, to avoid obstruction to other competitors. Should any competitor willfully impede a member of another team by running out of position or lane at the finishing stage, he is liable to cause the disqualification.

9. Assistance by pushing off or by any other method will cause disqualification.

10. Once a team has completed in the preliminary rounds of an event, the composition of the team must not be changed for any subsequent round or final, except on medical grounds duly certified by a medical officer appointed by the organizing committee.

CROSS COUNTRY RACES

Owing to the extremely varying circumstance in which cross country running is practiced through the world, especially regarding different seasons, climatic conditions and distances, it is impossible to legislate rigidly for international standardization of this sport.

The following rules, however, are intended as a guide and incentive to develop cross-country running, both as a sport in itself and as a training adjunct to track and field athletics.

1. The cross-country season should normally extend throughout the winter months after the close of the track and field season.

2. The course for championship and international events:

a) The race shall be run over a course which must be designed as an open or woodland area, covered as far as possible by grass, with natural obstacles; it should present itself as a challenging and interesting race course. The traversing of roads should be kept to a minimum.

b) The course shall be clearly marked, preferably with a fence or barriers on both sides. If this is not possible, at least, be clearly marked on both sides with a continuous tape.

c) When designing the course, very high obstacles should be avoided, so should deep ditches, dangerous ascent or descants, thick undergrowth and, in general any obstacle which would constitute a difficulty beyond the aim of competition.

Preferably no artificial obstacles should be used.

3. The course must be measured and the distance declared prior to the closing of entries.

4. Distance at IAFF World Cross Country Team Championships should be approximately :-

Category of athletes	**Long Course**	**Short Course**
Men	12Km	4Km
Women	8Km	4Km
Junior Men	8Km	-
Junior Women	6Km	-

It is recommended that similar distances are used for other International and National Competition.

5. The races shall be started by a gun-fire. Standard commands for distance events shall be used.

6. No competitor in cross-country event is allowed to receive assistance or refreshment or refreshment from any person during the progress of the race.

FIELD EVENTS

GENERAL CONDITIONS

1. At the competition arena and before the beginning of events, Athletes may have throwing events, the practice trial. The practice trials will be in draw order and always under the supervision of the judges.

2. Once or competition has begun, no Athlete shall be permitted to use the practice purpose, the run way of take off area, implements, the circles of the ground within sectors.

3. In all field events, where a runway is used, athlete is allowed to place markers alongside it except where markers can be placed on the runway. Markers shall be provided by the organizers. No markers shall be placed in any pit or landing area.

4. In field events, except the high jump and pole vault, where there are more than eight athletes, each athlete shall be allowed three trials and their best performance shall be allowed additional three trials. Where there are eight athletes or fewer,

each athlete shall be allowed six trials. In both cases, the competing order for the last three round shall be reverse order to the ranking reached after the first three trials.

5. Except for the high jump and pole vault, no athlete is allowed to have more than three trials recorded in any round of competition.

VERTICAL JUMPS:

General rules.

1. Lots drawn shall decide the other in which the competitors take these trials.
2. In all jumping event, the length of runway is unlimited. However, the minimum length provided for running high jump shall be 15meters and for other jumps, rom.
3. In all jumping events each competitor shall be executed with the best of all his jumps subject to condition relating to ties.
4. The employment of weights or grips of any kind is forbidden.
5. The take- off ground about the jump must be level.
6. Before the commencement of competition for height, the chief guest shall announce to the competitors the starting height and the different heights to which the far will be raised at the end of each round, until there is only one competitor remaining having won the competition or there is a tie for first place.
7. A competition may commence jumping at any height above the minimum height and may jump at any subsequent height. Three consecutive failures, regardless of the height at which any of such failures occur, disqualify him from further jumping/vaulting.

8. Unless there is only one competitor remaining.

   a) The bar should never be raised by less than 2 cm in the high jump and 5 cm in the pole vault after each round.

   b) The increment of the raising of the bar should never increase. In combined events competition held under rule 12, (b) and (c), each increase shall be uniformly 3 cm in the pole vault throughout the competition.

9. In the mattes of a tie, tie athletes with the lowest number of jumps at the tie height shall be awarded the highest place of the tie still persists, the athletes with the lowest total failures throughout the competition shall be placed higher.

HIGH JUMP

1. The competition shall take-off from one foot
2. A competition fails if:
    a) After the jump, the bar does not remain on the supports because of the action of the competition while jumping, or
    b) He touches the ground including the landing area beyond the place of the uprights with any part of his body, without first clearing the bar.
3. The upright or posts (of any style but rigid) shall not be moved during the competition unless the referee considers the take-off or landing ground has become unsuitable. In such cases the change shall be made only after a round has been completed.
4. It recommended that the landing area shall not be smaller than 6m x 4m x 0.7m.

POLE VAULT

1. The take-off for the pole vault shall be from a wooden or metal box, which shall be level with the ground.

2. In additional to the failure mentioned in general rule for jumping events given above, a competitor fail if he –

   a) Knocks the bar off the supports, or

   b) Leaves the ground for the purpose of making a vault and fails to clear the upper hand higher on the pole, or

   c) After leaving the ground places his lower hand above the upper one or moves the upper hand higher on the pole, or

d) Before taking off touches with any part of his body or the pole, the ground including landing area, beyond the plane of the stop-board of the wooden box.

e) Clear the bar but having relinquished is holding on the pole the lattes passed beneath the bar.

3. If in making an attempt the competitive pole is broken it shall not be counted as a failure.

4. No one shall be allowed to touch the pole unless it is falling away from the bar or upright, if it is so touched the vault shall be recorded as a failure.

5. Competitors may use their own poles.

6. No competitors shall be allowed to use any i=of the private poles except with the consent of the owner.

HORIZONTAL JUMP:

General Conditions.

1. In all horizontal jumping events, distance shall be recorded to the nearest 0.01m below the distance measured if the distance measured is not a whole centimeter.

2. The minimum length of the runway shall be 40m, with a width of 1.22m, and shall be marked by white lines 5cm in width.

LONG JUMP/TIPPLE JUMP

1. Drawing of lots for the trials and their order, the use of runway before competition etc. are governed by the general rules/conditions for jumping events, as given above

2. A competition fails if he-

   a) While taking off, touches the ground beyond the take off line with any part of his body, whether running up without jumping or in the act of jumping; or

   b) Takes off from outside and of the board, whether beyond or before the extension of the take-off line, or

   c) In the course of landing, touches the ground outside the landing area nearer to the take-off then the nearest break in the landing are made by the jump; or

d) After or completed jump, walks back through the landing area;

e) Or employs any form of so- while running up or in the act of jumping;

The take-off shall be from or board; the edge nearest to the landing area shall be called the scratch line, which will be placed between in and 3m from the nearer and of the landing area.

3. If a competitor takes off before reaching the scratch line, it shall not be counted, as a failure but the competitor shall be at a disadvantage for distance

4. Measurement shall be taken at right angles from the nearest break in the ground in the landing area (having a maximum width of 2.75m and a minimum of 3m) made by any part of the competitors body on the scratch line.

5. The triple jump shall consist of a hop, a step and a jump in that order (the rules for long jump shall apply in all order matters).

THROWING EVENTS

General rules

1. Lots shall draw the order in which the competitor take their trials.

2. Where there are more than eight competitors, each competitor shall be allowed three trials, and the eight competitors with the best valid performance shall be allowed three additional trials. In the events of a tie for eight places any competitor so tying shall be allowed three additional trials. Where there are eight competitors or fewer each competitor shall be allowed six trial.

3. In the competitions area, each competitor may have a maximum of two practice trials, which should be made in draw order under the supervision of the judges.

4. Once the competitions have begun, competitors are not permitted to use implements for practice purpose or to use the circle or ground within the sector for practice trials with or without implements.

5. All throws must be made from the circle. A competitor shall commence the throw from a stationary position.

6. In all throwing events from a circle or competitor is allowed to touch the inside of the iron band or stop board. It shall be a foul throw and not allowed to count if the competitor, after he has stopped into the circle and commenced to make a throw, touches with any part of his body the top of the stop board or circle or the ground outside or improperly releases the implement in making any attempts.

7. The competitor must not leave the circle until the implement has touches the ground, and he shall then, a standing position leave the circle from the rear half which shall be indicated by a chalk line drawn through the center and extended outside the circle not less than on each side.

8. The measurement of each throw shall be made from the nearest mark made by the fall of the implement (shot hammer, discuss or javelin) to the inside of the circle (or the arc in case of javelin) along a lane from the mark made by the implement to the center of the circle or the center of the radius of the arc.

9. Only throwing implements provided by the organizers of the meets shall be used. No competitor is permitted to take any implements into the arena. No modification shall be made to any implements during the competition.

10. No device of any kind example-typing of two or more fingers together, which in any ways assist, shall be allowed.

11. In all throwing events implements must be carried back to the starting line or circle and thrown back.

12. In all International competitions, the implements used shall comply with IAAF specifications. The following table shows the weight of each implements used by each age group.

Implements	**Women Youth/Junior/Senior**	**Men Youth**	**Men Junior**	**Men Senior**
Shot-put	4.00 Kg	5.000 Kg	6.00 Kg	7.260 Kg
Discuss	1.000 Kg	1.5000 Kg	1.750 Kg	2.000 Kg
Hammer	4.000 Kg	5.000 Kg	6.000 Kg	7.260 Kg
Javelin	600 Gm	700 Gm	800 Gm	800 Gm

SHOT PUT

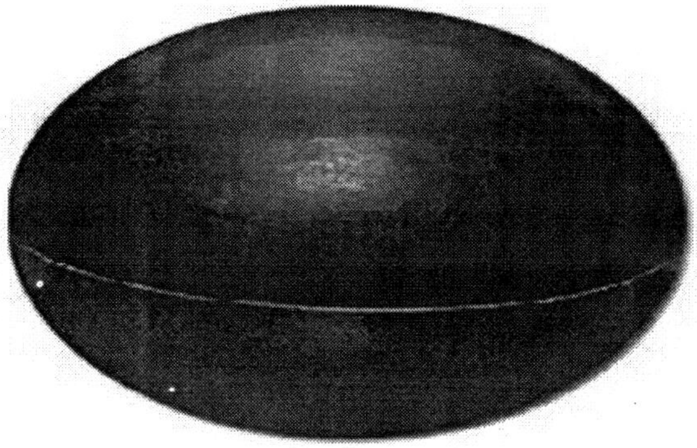

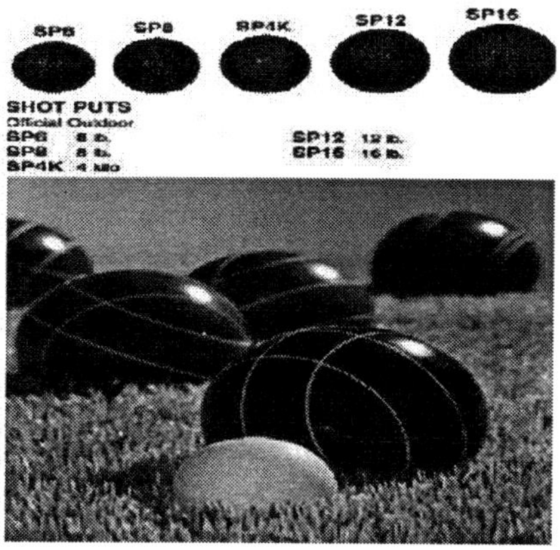

1. The shot put shall be put from a circle the inside diameter of which shall be 2.135m (+-5mm). The rim of the circle shall be at least than 6mm thick and shall be white.

2. A white line 5cm wide shall be drawn from the top of the metal ream extending for at least 75cm on either side of the circle. It may be painted or made of wood or other suitable materials. The rear edge of the white line shall from a prolongation of a theoretical line through the center line of the landing sector.

3. The shot (for senior men and women) shall conform to the following specification.

Specification of shot	**Men**	**Women**
Minimum weight acceptance of a record	7.260 kg	4.000 kg

Range for supplying of equipment	7.265 kg	4.005
	7.285 kg	4.025 kg
Minimum diameter	110 mm	95 mm
Maximum diameter	130 mm	110 mm

4. The shot (solid, iron, brass or any metal ball) shall be put from the shoulder with one hand only. At the time competition takes the stance in the circle to commence a put; the shot shall touch or be in proximity to the chin and the hand shall be not dropped below this position during the action of putting. The shot shall not be taken behind the line of the shoulder.

5. All measurements shall be made immediately after each throw.

DISCUSS THROW

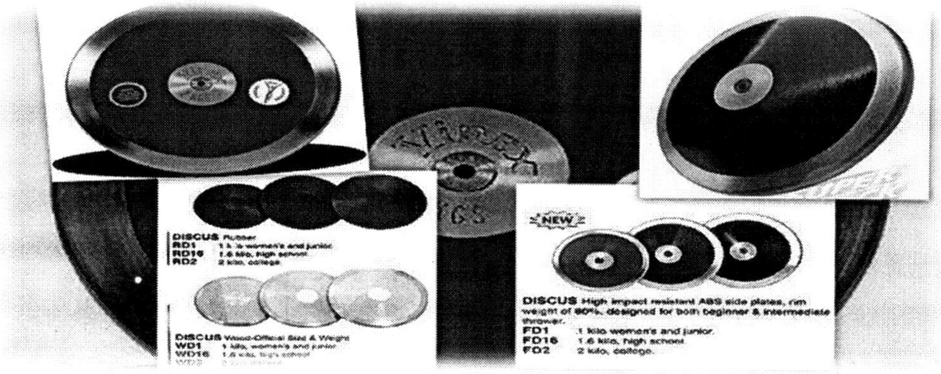

1. The discus shall be thrown from a circle of the inside diameter of which shall be 2.50 m (±5mm). The rim of the circle shall be at least 6 mm thick and shall be white.

2. The body of the discus shall be made of wood, or other suitable material, with a metal rim, the edge of which shall be circular. The cross section of the edge shall be rounded in a tree circle having a radius of approximately 6 mm. Each side of the discus shall be identical and shall be made without indentations, projections or sharp edges. The side shall taper in a straight line from the beginning of the curve of the rim to a circle of a radius of 25 mm to 28.5 mm from the center of the discus (for senior men and women) shall conform to the following specifications:

Specifications of Discus	**Men**	**Women**
Weight	2 kg	1 kg
Minimum for acceptance of a round	2.005 kg	1.005 kg
Range for supply of equipments for competitions	2.025 kg	1.025 kg

Outside diameter of metal rim (min)	219 mm	180 mm
(Max)	221 mm	182 mm
Diameter of metal plate of flat centre area (min)	50 mm	50 mm
(max)	57 mm	57 mm
Thickness over flat centre area (min)	44 mm	37 mm
(max)	46 mm	39 mm
Thickness of rim (min)	12 mm	12 mm
(max)	13 mm	13 mm

3. The competitions may adopt any position of throw as per his convenience.

4. For a valid throw the discus must fall so that the points from which measurement is to be made is within the inner edges of lines marking a sector of 34.92° set out all the ground so that the radii level cross at the centre of the circle.

5. All discus throw shall be made from an enclosure or lays to ensure safety of spectator, officials, and athletes.

HAMMER THROW

1. All throws shall be made from the circle 2.135 m in diameter with 5 mm ± allowance. The rim of the circle shall be at least 6 mm thick and shall be white.

2. A white line 5 cm wide shall be drawn from the top of the metal rim either side of the circle. It may be painted or made of wood or other suitable material. The rear line through the center of the circle at right angles to the center line of the landing sector. The hammer (which is made of a metal head, a wire of a handle) may be thrown from the discus circle provided the diameter of this circle is reduced from 2.50m to 2.135m by placing a circle ring inside.

3. When throwing the hammer, ordinary gloves for protecting of the hand are permitted.

4. The competitor in his starting position pear to the preliminary swings or terms is allowed to put the head of the hammer or the ground outside the circle.

5. It shall not be considered a foul through if the head of the hammer touches the ground when the competition makes the preliminary swings or term s; but if, after having so touched the ground, he stops throwing so as to begin the throw again, this shall count as a failure.

6. The competitor may adopt any position for initial stance.

7. Immediately after throw all measurement should be made.

8. A hammer throws shall be made from an enclosure or cage to ensure safety of spectators, officials and athletes.

9. For a valid through the hammer must fall so that the point from which measurement is to be made within the inner edges of lines marking a sector of approximately 34.92 degree set out on the ground so that the radii line touch with their edges the extremities of the stop board and cross at centre of the circle.

10. If the hammer breaks during a throw or while in the air, it shall not count as a throw provided it was in accordance with the rules. If the competitor loses his equipment's and commits a foul, it shall not count against him.

JAVELIN THROW

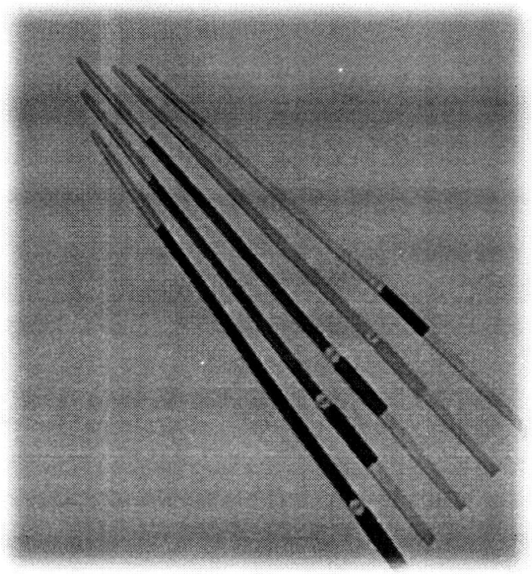
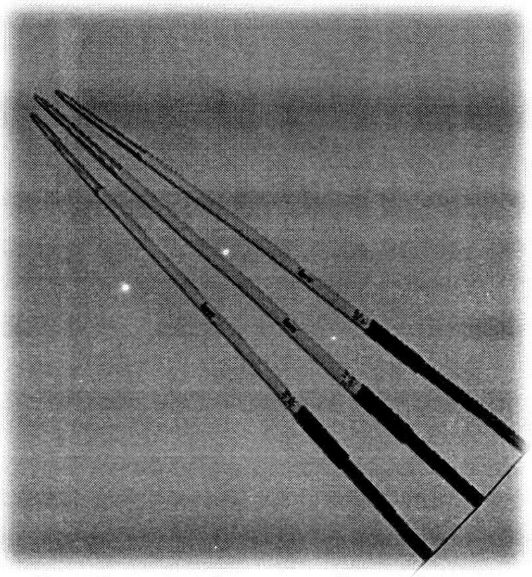

1. The length of the runway shall not be more than 36.5m and not less than 30m and shall be marked by two parallel lines 5cm in width and 4m apart. The throw shall be made from behind an arc of a circle drawn with a radius of 8m; such arc shall consist of a strip made of wood or metal 7cm wide painted white and such flush with the ground lines shall be drawn from the extremities of the arc at right angles to the parallel lines marking the runway. This line shall be 1.50m in length and 7cm in width.

2. The javelin shall be held at the grip. It shall be thrown over the shoulder or upper part of the throwing arm and shall not be slung or hurled. Non-orthodox style is not permitted.

3. A throw shall be valid only if the tip of the metal head strikes the ground before any part of the javelin.

4. At no time during the throw, until the javelin has been discharged into the air, may the competitor turn completely around, so that his back is toward the throwing arc.

5. It shall be a foul throw if the competitor, after he has started his throw, touches with any part of his body or limbs, the line de-marking, or the ground outside, the running or improperly releases the javelin in making any attempt.

6. All throws to be valid must fall within the inner edges of lines making the sector set out on the ground.

7. It shall be a foul throw if the competitor, after he has started his throws, touches with part of his body or limbs the lines making the runway or the ground outside the runway or improperly released the javelin in making an attempt.

8. The javelin (for senior men and women) shall confirm to the following specifications.

Specific action of javelin	**Men**	**Women**
Weight (inclusive of cord grip)	800 gm	600 gm
Range for supply of equally for competition overall length	805-825 gm	605-625 gm
	Min 2.60m	2.20m
	Max 2.70m	2.30m
Length of metal head	Min 250 mm	250mm
	Max 330mm	330mm

Distance from trip of metal head to cord grip	Min 0.90m	0.80m
	Max1.60m	0.95m
Width of cord grip	Min 150mm	140mm
	Max 160mm	150mm

SKILLS AND TECHNIQUES OF SELECTED ATHLETIC EVENTS SPRINTING

Sprinting is one of the oldest rewarded forms of athletic competition. To begin with the ancient Olympic Games consisted almost entirely of sprint races. At that time all athletes irrespective of their body size were supposed to use standard blocks of marble with grove. In due course of time, as same, a few earlier references reveal, sprint races were held between the servants of the mobility. Sprinting is marked by intense body action and high speed and is runway at or near maximum speed as long as possible for distances and including 100m and 400m. All sprinting events commence with a crouch start.

Further, 100m (or less) is called short sprint, 200m is known as medium sprint and 400m is known as long sprint run respectively by a poor sprints, a natural sprinter and an endurance sprinter.

CROUCH START TECHNIQUE:

"On your marks"

"Set"

"Go"

Introduces in 1887 by Sherrill, crouch start, is used in all running events up to 400m. It allows the runner, through proper positioning of his centre of gravity in the 'set' position, to respond quickly to the gun and start the race.

The crouch is further classified into bunch or bullet start, medium start, and elongated start largely differing blocks and the distance from the blocks to the starting line.

BUNCH OR BULLET START

In this start, both feet are close together making a short of bunch. The front block is placed 19 to 24 inches back of the starting line and the front block. 10 to 12 inches behind the front block. The runner takes position on the toe of his back fort and the heel of his front foot an aligned.

The angles of inclination of the blocks must guarantee or good push off, i.e. they must permit full pressure of the ball each foot against the surface of each block. However this kind of start has not been found suitable for young and beginners.

MEDIUM START:

In medium start, the distance between the front and the rear block is approximately 16-20 inches. The athlete places the front foot 12-15 inches anyway from the starting line. The rear front is placed so that the knee of the rear leg is placed on the ground alongside and level with the toe of the leading foot. The hands are placed up to the starting line slightly more than shoulder width apart. This position produces a somewhat higher initial speed than the bunch start, mainly due to a better distribution of body weight over the limbs in the 'set' position.

The technique produces over-all best results. Therefore, the novices and hurdlers should be taught this as a fundamental crouch starting.

ELONGATED START:

The distance between the two blocks is approximately 24-28 inches the one between the front foot and the starting line 13 inches or so. Obviously the front foot relatively very closed to the starting line whereas the rear foot is far away from it. This is the least effective of the three starts. The young untutored athletes after adapt it.

TAKING A START:

As per rule, taking a start involves three fundamental positions. "On your marks", "Set" and "Gun Shot" or "Go". Importing check points for each of them are given below.

ON YOUR MARK:

1. Front foot between 16 to 24 inches from the line.
2. Back foot approximately 16 inches behind the front foot. The front foot should be level with the knee of the rear leg.
3. Shoulders vertically over the hands.

4. The tips of the fingers from a supporting bridge just behind the line, after using the second joint of the fingers.

5. The head is still in natural alignment with the body. The weight spread evenly between the supporting points.

6. The rear knee is about three inches to the right of the front foot.

SET:

1. At the command, the knee is lifted from the ground, so that both legs are semi-flexed.

2. The angle at the front knee is about 90° and at the rear knee, approximately 120°.

3. The hips rise somewhat higher than the shoulders.

4. The shoulders are only slightly ahead of the heads.

5. The head is still, in natural alignment with the body. The arms are kept well extended, with weight spread evenly between the supporting points.

6. The eyes are still focused on a points about one meter down the track.

GUN SHOT/GO:

1. In a reflex action, the athletic drives against the blocks, at the same time lifting his arm from the ground and through a vigorous arm use, produces an imbalance which will initiate the starting action.

2. Fast and vigorous forward and upward drive of the right leg (rear foot on the block)

3. Full extension of the left leg from the head through the body to the driving foot.

4. There is virtually a straight line from the head through the body to the driving foot.

5. Body is kept low.

6. The head is still in natural alignment with the body. There should be no tendency to throw the head back or to touch the chin out the chest.

MECHANICS OF A FULL SPRINTING ACTION

RUNNING RESULT:

The sprinting must run fall:

- Body and head correctly aligned.
- Relaxation no rigidity,
- Chin in, chest out, abdomen in, tail in, shoulders down, knees straight ahead, feet slightly apart and pointing forward.
- Arms relaxed at the side.
- Body weight balanced towards the back of the feet.
- In running, the same alignment is maintained to the runner weight over the balls of the feet.

ARM ACTION:

With lower arm at an angle of 90° with the upper arm, the athlete should attain a powerful device backwards with the arms, aiming for high elbows for power thrust. The position of the hands at the front of the body should not come higher than the shoulders forward thrust is a reflex action as a result of backward power thrust.

An addition to assisting the legs to do their work the arms also help to cancel out unwanted rotation caused by the leg action.

LEG ACTION:

There are two essentials to a diff and completing of drive. The front should land slightly ahead of the body and then a forward drive should be taken. The drive must drive must then be completed in that the driving leg must be fully extended behind the body before being recovered.

The athlete should be encouraged to run tall by keeping the hips high. The trunk should be kept slightly forward or vertical. The angle of the body at any given movement depends on the acceleration rate.

MIDDLE AND LONG DISTANCE RACES

As per rules, the start in middle and long distance races is invariably from a standing position that is less complicated than the crouch start in sprint events. In the dynamics and mechanics of running, the two types of races also differ significantly. The sprints are speed based events, the middle and long distance races require tremendous speed endurance and stamina. After the pistol shot, the athlete body should adopt a body lean in order to assist stretching movement of the legs and, in particular, the forward awing of the leg. Body lean is function of acceleration. Here the economy of energy is the most important consideration. All wasteful, hindering movements must be excluded by the use of rotational technique.

GOOD RUNNING MECHANISM:

A good running mechanism aims to achieve a balanced movement of the body parts, and is invariably characterized by the following:

1. The torso is erect. There is very little forward lean except during acceleration. The athlete must run tall with the hips forward.

2. The foot should touchdown directly under the torso. The position of the foot as it touches down varies widely among the running.

3. The legs move through drive, recovery and support phases. Distance runner use less knee lift and recovery leg-kick then sprinters.

4. The arm are used for balanced and to transfer momentum, as in accelerating or running up a hill. The arm is carried at about a 90 degree angle, swinging freely from the shoulders. They should not cross the mid-line of the body. The aggressiveness of the arms movements is directly related to speed. The hands are cupped or curled comfortably, palm facing inward the middle of the body.

5. The position of the head should be relatively level. The runner should look about to 20m to 30m ahead. Some runner look just below the horizon they are running. The base of the neck and shoulder should be relaxed also.

FINISHING A RACE:

Finishing a race is a important as starting because it determines the position of an athlete in the content. Generally, there are three techniques used by athletes to finish the race. Run through, lunge and shoulder shrug. In running through the athlete to run at the acceleration rate of speed and breast the tape without making any special movement. The keeps his gaze 5-10 ahead of the finishing line and remains as natural as possible in his movements. In lunge technique the athlete stops forward when the finish line is just one step ahead. He breasts the tape on the finish line, keeping his arms bent and backwards. In shoulder shrug, the athlete shrugs forward either of the shoulder and the same side arm so as to touch the tape, keeping the other shoulder and arm backwards downwards.

Adoption of a finishing technique is a matter of convenience rather than any hard and fast rule.

RELAYS

Unlike simple sprints, relay (usually 4x100 and 4x400m) are team events in which four runners (of each team) run in tendon the prescribed distance. They exchange the baton with the exchange zone. Relays are characterized by an intense team sprint and a highly co-ordinate action. The most technical aspect of a relay is baton pass, which is effected by any of the following method.

DOWNWARD PASS:

In this pass, the outgoing runner extends the receiving hands back palm up with the thumb towards the body. The incoming runner holds the baton by one end and places the free end in the hand of the outgoing runner. The three advantages of this pass are free distance between the runner at the exchange (the incoming runner never catches up with the outgoing runner) the batons needs no adjustment in the hand after the pass (it is ready for the next speed. The disadvantage is the possibility of a moving target prevented by the outgoing runner.

UP-WARD PASS:

In this pass, the outgoing runner holds receiving hands in an upside down "V" positions the baton so that incoming runners to learn the disadvantage is that baton needs adjustment and creates greater risk of dropping the baton. Another disadvantage is that some incoming runner tends to overcome the outgoing runner.

SNATCH PASS:

The snatch pass is identical to the downward pass at the point of exchange. The incoming runner holds the baton forward, using the outgoing runner's elbow as a target. The outgoing runner reaches back and grasps the baton. If the pass is missed on the first try the outgoing runner continues normal arm swing motion and grabs the baton on the second back swing.

IMPORTANT CONSIDERATION IN RELAYS:

The goal of all relays into move the baton around the track as fast as possible. The following elements shoulder be kept in mind before the competition.

RELAY ORDER:

Many factors are considered is arranging a relay team's running order such as the west (fastest most reliable) starts, the best turn runners, the best baton handlers, each athletes overall speed and ability to sustain speed etc. competitiveness of an athlete and experience level of the team-mates, psychological and anthropometrical values should also be kept in mind before deciding the relay order.

USE OF ACCELERATION ZONE:

The acceleration zone sets the outgoing runner accelerates properly. Depending upon the athletics ability the coach should decide the use of exchange zone.

STARTING POSITION OF THE OUTGOING RUNER:

The out-going runner should take up a good starting position. The runner may stand facing forward, learning in a balanced position, with the rear-foot on the same side as the receiving arm. He/she then looks over the shoulder of the receiving arm, which is forward with the hips and feet in the direction of the run, for the incoming runner.

ESTABLISHING THE GO MARK:

This mark tells the outgoing runner when to begin accelerating. When the incoming runners take off, the relative speed of both runners in the exchange determines the marks placement.

TAKE OFF AND ACCELERATION:

The outgoing runner must learn to be patient. Taking off too early can lead to deserts. The outgoing runner should be in a pre-learning position before the incoming runner reaches the 'go' marks. Once begun, the acceleration of the outgoing runner must be consistent. Changing acceleration patterns leads to timing problems.

ESTABLISH THE EXCHANGE POINT WITHIN THE ZONE:

The athlete should practice exchange towards the middle of a zone until they have a good feet of their ability. After choosing the relay team the exchange points can be moved forward or backward.

SIGNALING THE EXCHANGE:

The incoming runner can signal the exchange with verbal commands at specific points when he/she is ready to pass the baton. The runner should use unusual words or distinctive signal- a crisp, loud, distinguishable command and remember that up to eight other athletes will be shouting at the same time.

VISUAL EXCHANGE TECHNIQUE FOR THE 4X400M RELAY

Visual changes are used because of the nature of the distance run, the incoming athlete is very tired at the time of the exchange and his main responsibility is to hold the batten upwards or vertical in the right hand to give outgoing runner a clear view in the crowed zone.

In the visual exchange as the responsibility for the change shifts on to the outgoing runner, he adjusts his speed to the incoming runner to achieve maximum free space take the baton, accelerates and fights to maintain the advantage of the inside position going into the turn. There are three accepted methods for visual pass in longer relays, the outside exchange, the inside exchange and the mixed method. The most prevalent technique is the mixed method i.e. right to left exchange for all three exchanges. This position allows the outgoing runner to face the infield and to see where the traffic is. The outgoing runner should switch the baton from the left to the right hand as soon as possible after establishing a forward run.

The outgoing runner must gauge the aped he/she needs to have accomplished. The exchange takes place near the middle of the zone, not allowing the baton to slow down.

It is better for the receiver to gradually accelerate while moving forward the mid zone, accelerating at the points of exchange than having to slow down. The receiver waits for the baton with a hip and foot position similar to that in the 4x400m but only with a sight lean.

Once the incoming runner reaches a point that the outgoing runner considers a signal to leave, the outgoing runner turn the head and eyes to the front for three strides. Then he looks and reaches back with the receiving hands at the third stride to adjust his or her speed to match that exchange should maintain the baton speed.

HURDLING

Through not of the classical Greek world like the javelin or the discus, huddling a creation of the 19th century is one of the most fascinating areas of track and field fascinating areas of track and field as it encompasses both running and field events. Modern hurdling involves running fast over ten obstacles.

Rhythm, balance and smoothness are key factors in hurdling. Leg and arm action are per liar to this event.

LEADING LEG:

Special attention must be given to the action of the lead that consists of a quick forward and upward thrust of the leading leg in the direction of the hurdle edge and the active downward pressing of the thigh immediately after clearance for the landing. In the sequence of actions, the head should be kept straight with no twist or aversion of the lead foot and leading with the knee in jack knife action that brings the chest dawn on the thigh. The knee is not locked.

ARM ACTION INTO THE HURDLE:

The arm action in the hurdle is more forceful than in sprinting. As the knee is driven up and the opposite arm and shoulder reach forward and down. The shoulder should be kept square to the hurdle and no attempt should be made to touch the toe.

THE TRAIL LEG ACTION:

The trail leg is delayed to gain a full split of the legs and forward drive in at the hurdle. It comes flat or just above the horizontal plane as it crosses the hurdle. The toes are kept high to avoid snagging the hurdle. Beyond the hurdle bring the knee high with no loss or forward lean of the torso to reach out for a full stride.

KEY CONCEPTS FOR EFFICIENT FAST HURDLE:

- "Attack" the first hurdle gets there first and don't "set" for the hurdle.
- Hips high in approaching and running of each hurdle.
- A fast lead leg led by a flexed knee.
- Driving across the hurdle with a low trajectory, maintaining horizontal velocity, throughout the race. Not only over the hurdles but between them as well.
- Keep all limbs moving across the hurdle rear leg should be swept through strongly and a vigorous opposite arm/rear leg action should be encouraged.
- Keep body, particularly shoulders, square to the hurdle with no twisting or less of balance.

DISCUSS THROW

TECHNIQUE:-

To obtain maximum distance in throwing the discus, a sequence of movements involving forward acceleration acquired through body rotation with the discus held at arm's length must occur.

THE GRIP:

Grasping the discus depends on the size of the hand. Desirable, the discus is held flat against the palm with the first joint of each finger over the edge. The fingers are slightly and evenly spread and grasp the edge firmly.

THE INITIAL STANCE:

The competitor stands at the back of the circle with the feet at approximately right angle to the direction of the throw. The body weight is even distributed between the feet. The trunk is almost erect depending on knee bent. The musculature is relaxed and initial stance is flat footed.

THE PRELIMINARY SWING:

Usually, the competitor swing the discus from front to back three times for the purpose of establishing proper balance, reassuring himself of his grasps, and adding impetus to his body for the beginning of the turn.

THE PIVOT ON THE FOOT:

When last preliminary swing reaches the fastest point back, the competitor's body weight is on the right foot (for right hand throwers) while body balance is maintains by contact of the ball of the left foot with the ground. The knees are slightly bent. As discus is brought forward the trunk is turned is turned shapely to the left and body weight is shifted from right to the left foot.

THE PIVOT:

Maintaining the impetus against the imbalance in the half turn, the competitor continues the turn by shifting the body-weight on to the right foot and executes an additional half turn by pivoting on the right. During the turn the left foot reaches ahead toward the front of the circle and establishes conduct with the ground. The player finally turns into the position for final effort.

THE DELIVERY :

With both feet on the ground and body-weight mainly on right foot, the competitor throws himself into the final heave that involves the execution. It should be initiated with a vigorous forward-upward thrust of right hip, straightening of the right leg, a rapid twist of the trunk to the left, an explosive whip of the arm and a fast powerful snap of the wrist, which had previously been 'set' or cocked for this moment.

THE RELEASE:

The discus is released with the plane of the throw at an angle of approximately 30' and is released from a point about opposite or slightly ahead of the shoulder. It leaves hand, spinning in a clockwise direction. The spin is brought about by the follow through of the arm and is given additional impetus by the vigorous snap of the wrist to the left. As the discuss is released, the momentum of the body tends to carry the thrower forward and since he must stay within the circle, he must gain body-balance.

THE RECOVERY:

After the discus is released, the body-weight is totally on the right foot.

Balance is gained by synchronizing the bending on the right knee and the backward swinging of the left leg and left arm.

SHOT PUT

Putting the shot is an event which seems to have had its origin in putting the stone, and came to be practiced in Ireland and Scotland as a pastime.

TECHNIQUE:

The aim of technique is to add impetus to the shot by body shift across the circle. From the beginning to the end of the put, there are a number of well-defined movements such as holding the shot, taking initial stance, glide, putting movement, delivery, release etc.

The shot is put, not thrown.

Traditionally there are two techniques of putting the shot:

The Rational Technique or Disco put, and the Glide Technique. Most competitors use the gliding technique. The movements in orders of which they are executed are illustrated.

THE INITIAL STANCE:

For a right hand putter, the right foot is close to the back edge of the circle and left foot 10 to 16 inches away from the circle. The angle, direction and distance of placement depends upon the convenience of the putter.

The shot is carried slightly above and directly in front of the shoulder with the elbow away from the body. In the initial stance, the right knee supporting most of the body weight is slightly bent. The left hand is extended upward and outward in order to balance. Except the hand grasping the shot, body musculature is, in general, relaxed.

THE LEG SWING:

For the purpose of securing poise and balance for the shift, the putter performs preliminary leg swings. These swings may be executed by swinging the left leg forward and backward in line with the right leg. The type of preliminary swing employed rests with the putter. As the left foot reaches the further most point back, the shift begins.

THE SHIFT:

At the beginning of the shift, the body-weight is on right leg, with right knee moderately bent. As the left foot reaches the most forward point in the swing, the right leg is vigorously straightened at the right thigh, leg and foot give moderate push. The movement desired is a low glide. At the completion of the shift the left foot lands near the toe board. The feet are fairly wide spread. In this position the body-weight rests chiefly on the right foot, and the right shoulder is drawn well back. From this position, there are summation of all forces of the body to provide forward propulsion of the shot.

THE DELIVERY:

As soon as the feet are planted after the shift, the delivery begins. An effective put is one in which there is no pause between shift and delivery. During the course of delivery there is straightening and rotation of the right leg, a quick twist of the trunk to the left, a forceful push of the right arm upward and forward, a forceful swing of the left elbow to the left side and backward and a push off from the right toe.

THE RELEASE:

The total of all forces generated in shift and the delivery has been transmitted to the wrist and fingers. In addition to these forces there is instantaneous forward snap of the wrist and flip of the fingers.

THE RECOVERY:

The right foot is flush against the toe board while the left leg is swung backward and sideward. To avoid even the appearance of a foul, the competitor is urged to retire from the circle by way of the rear half.

JAVELIN THROW

The javelin throw has been evolved into its present form from an accident practice of throwing a spear for either distance or accuracy.

TECHNIQUE:

Javelin technique has undergone significant changes in the course of its development. In its latest form, it comprises the following technical elements:

THE GRIP:

The type of grip depends on the length and strength of the fingers, the size of the javelin shaft, and the athlete's personal choice.

a) Finnish hold: It consists of grasping of the javelin at the rear of the binding so that the second finger encircles the shaft and barely touches the extended thumb. The first finger is approximately in line with the wrist and curls slightly around the shaft.

b) American grip: The javelin is held with three fingers encircling the whip-yard and thumb resting lightly along the shaft.

c) Hungarian form. The shaft lies in the hand hummock in a manner similarly to the Finnish style. The first finger is extended to the rear along the underside of the shaft.

CARRYING THE JAVELIN:

The type of carry selected by a competitor depends on the ease with which he can fit into the run, the drawing back of the arm, and the delivery.

THE APPROACH:

The run is started from a spot that is located at the distance of 100 to110 feet from the spot board (scratch line). During the approach the javelin is carried to the front. The thrower does not hold it in a stationary manner but moves it up and down, synchronizing the right arm action with the left leg action.

THE DELIVERY RELEASE AND THE RECOVERY:

The movement involved in delivery usually involves five steps. On count 1, the right foot strikes the ground in the direction of the board. On count 2, the left foot pointed to the right strikes the ground. On count 3, the right foot executes a front crossover step landing with the toe pointed to the right and the right foot parallel to the board. On count 4, an extremely long step is taken, the left foot landing in the direction of the throw. When the right foot touches the ground and a step preceding the throw, the whole body is inclined backward about 35° to 40°. When the feet stop momentarily on the ground, the centre of weight continues forward, forcing the top of the body practically to double its forward speed. On count 1, the javelin point is tilted upward. On count 2, the arm is straightened and thrust forward. The javelin is lowered and is approximately parallel with the ground.

At count 3, the throwing arm is drawn completely back. At count 4, initiation of throw occurs, the elbow leads the hand. The arm action is such that the shaft when released forms an angle of 35° with the ground. The javelin is released just above and slightly in front of the right shoulder.

In recovery, the use of the arms in maintaining balance is an individual characteristic.

HAMMER THROW

TECHNIQUE:

The hammer throwing technique has considerably improved over time. It is determine by the specific nature of the implement and the measurement of the throwing circle. Crucial for the length of flight of the implement is initial velocity that is created by preliminary swings or winds.

STARTING POSITION:

The athlete stands in the rear half of the circle with his back facing the direction of the throw; the feet are shoulder-width apart. Balanced stance, knees slightly bent, back straight, head up, eyes looking forward. The thrower holds the handle of the hammer with the second joint of the gloved left hand and the right hand covers the left with the thumb crossed over the right. He reaches back to place the hammer in its starting position for the initial swing.

WINDS:

The purpose of the winds is to create the centrifugal force (building up momentum) that is needed to convert the throwers mass into force as he begins to rotate with the hammer in the turns. The thrower should speed up the hammer when it is going downward. The speed of the movement is increased gradually from first move of the hammer throw each cycle.

THE TURNS:

The purpose of this turns is to develop and increase the velocity of the ball. As the thrower moves through the turns, he should note how the hammer feels while it is under control. The body weight moves successively from the left foot (displacement) to a position between both (double-support).

DIRECTION OF THE FEET ADVANCEMENT:

In the modern day's technique of hammer throwing, the direction of the feet advance through the circle is not parallel to the throwing direction but at an angle of 10 degree to 20 degree to the throwing direction, the thrower's right foot lands earlier, which bring the hammer around sooner. This allows the thrower to apply force from a higher point to a lower point through a longer path. The force exerted on the hammer is the result of the acceleration produced during the turns and is increased with the final movement which begins in the double support position- a very rapid rotation of the lower and upper body followed by a forceful extension of legs and trunk.

DELIVERY:

As the ball reaches maximum velocity at approximately 135degree, it is pulled from the thrower's grip and flies away. It is at this movement that the ball and its centripetal force finally wins over the thrower's body mass and its centripetal force and begins its flight through space.

LONG JUMP

The long (or running broad) jump, as an event on the track and field programmed can be traced to the ancient Olympic Games where it was one of the first regular event.

TECHNIQUE:

As a performing event, long jump consists of four phases – the run-up or approach, the take-off, the flight, and landing which blend together for the total movement.

THE APPROACH:

The run-up consists of three phases: the entry phase (commencing approach from a check mark located on the side of the runway); the central phase (where the athlete builds up rhythms and develops optimum speed), and; the preparation for take-off. The run-up involves developing a stride plan. So, the style of approach the athlete adopts shall depend on whether momentum is gained slowly, fairly fast or extremely fast. Basically there are three plans for stride adjustments: the 2-4-8 stride plan. The 2-4-6, and the 2-4-10-stride plan. It takes sometime before the beginners become expert in selecting their stride plan most suitable to their physical attributes.

- For beginners, the most consistent method of entry is a standing start
- The athlete runs tall (head, shoulder, hips in line
- High knee lift
- Powerful but relaxed arm drive
- Full extension of the driving leg
- Relaxation while accelerating towards optimum speed
- Increase leg speed in the final stride of the run-up
- Adjust body angle, keeping more upright posture than that of a sprinter
- The last stride is made fast with a firm flat-footed plant, slightly ahead of the body, in the line of the jump.

THE TAKE OFF:

The phase of long is also called "the foot-stamp", or "pound the board", which indicates that the jumper strikes the board flat footed and then applies vigorous effort to the board. In no case is the take-off board to be slapped lightly. For the proper take-off the centre of gravity should be slightly ahead of the point of the application of the power. The aped-stamp force must be combined in both upward and forward propulsion with the emphasis on the stamp. The jumper should stride the take-off board flat-footed. This is accomplished principally by shortening the last stride. If the take-off is not completely straightened, valuable power in the sprint is lost.

Note the following features:

- A vertical alignment of the head, upper body and hips.
- A vigorous drive with the knee of the free leg to hip level (the free leg is bent at the knee, with the foot trailing behind).
- A vigorous arm drive coordinated with drive.
- Complete extension of the take-off leg at hip, knee and ankle joints.

THE FLIGHT:

When the contact with the take-off board is broken, the flight through the air starts. In flight there are two principal concerns for the jumper. First, some means of movement should be employed to help prevent unwanted forward rotation. Second, there ought to be some action to provide an effective landing.

There are three distinct type of flight through the air: (a) the walk-with-the-air (hitch kick), (b) the hang style, and (c) the knee tuck type. (this is generally used as it increases forward rotation).

The hang style of jump is very appropriate and largely used for the beginners. In this style, after the take-off, the jumper allows his swinging leg to drop until it almost reaches the vertical line, where it is jointed by the flexed take-off leg. The lower leg parts of both legs are close together at a right angle with the thighs. The arms are brought to an overhead position with as much back-arch as possible thus delaying forward rotation. The jumper's body travels half the jumper distance in this position. For landing, he lifts both legs upward and forward and lowers the trunk in a balancing movement. Just before touching the ground, the jumper thrust his calves well forward.

The hitch-kick is most effective style in which he jumper actually continues to run in the air. He performs two and a half strides in the mid-air, where a secondary rational axis with the arms is established to absorb small amount of forward rotation. The hitch-kick is described as an almost continual cycling or wind-milling of the arms and legs while in flight – more simply, one and a half to two steps in the air.

LANDING:

As the action in air ceases, the athlete benefits by arising and extending the legs as completely as possible. At the time the head is forceful brought down to the thighs. The arms work in conjunction with the head, swinging from behind and over the top down and past the legs.

When the feet have contacted the pit, both arms are brought forceful to keep the athlete from falling backward. Whether landing will be in a "sitting" or tucked-in position depends on the ability of the athlete.

Mark the following two important feature of landing:

- The landing is made with the feet together, around the body.
- The knees bend on contact to allow the body to move beyond the foot marks.

HIGH JUMP

Like long jump, high also consists of fours phases: the run-up, the take-off, the flight and bar clearance, and landing. Even though several techniques of high jump over the decades, the jump phases remain the same.

HIGH-JUMPING STYLE:

The earliest technique used in high jump was Scissors Style – so natural and still so popular with novice for it does not involve much complicated learning. Then followed the eastern cut-off and the western roll – also known as the Straddle Style, which remained very popular with most world-class athletes until Dick Fosbery introduced Fosbery Flop Style at the 1968-Olympic in Maxico.

The scissor style may be good for the beginners, but it is of little use to any athlete worth the name. Similarly, neither the Eastern Cut-off nor the Western Roll style of high-jumping is practiced anywhere in the world.

The straddle style is still in use at the lower levels of athletic competitions. In this, the take-off foot is nearest to the bar, the jumper faces the bar and lands on the other foot; he runs 5 to 9 strides to speed up and approach the bar at 35degree to 45degree. The last stride is comparatively longer, the take-off foot touching the take-off point in heel-ball-toe action, with the take-off leg being kicked upward direction. The landing may be on shoulder(s) or back depending upon the torque.

The traditional Eastern Cut-off, the Western Roll and the Straddle Styles of jumping have the following common features, as shown in the figure:

- Co-ordination of approach and take-off with the simultaneous drive of the free leg upward and strong action.
- Rotation over the bar and clearance aided by the co-ordinate movements of the body segments. Dropping of the arms and shoulders, aiming at rotation with the help of the take-off leg.

FOSBERY FLOP:

The purpose of the approach is more than simply running to the bar and taking off. Most often approach in flopping is that of a "J" shape. Since it is beginning in a straight line, it allows for the development of speed build-up, and transferred to the slight curve at the end (usually 3 to 5 steps in length). The approach length is gradually 9-11 strides.

- The first step sets the tempo of the whole approach. This step should be measured, marked and practiced.
- Step 2-5 are in straight line. The body-position of the jumper should be balanced. The body should be over the foot when it contacts the ground. The jumper must not be leaning forward in an attempt to accelerate.

- The curve, "turn mark", should always be placed on the approach-surface during practice. This mark enables the jumper to develop awareness of when to change the approach and start to "lean-in" on the curve and build his centripetal force.
- The last three strides of final strides going into-take off must now change. These strides must be smooth and quick. Acceleration at the approach allows the jumper to actually the strides length slightly.

THE PLANTS:

The outside foot should be planted almost parallel to the bar pointing the opposite standard. The plant should be heal-to-toe action.

ARM ACTION:

On the second to last (penultimate) stride, the arm should gather and synchronize with what will be the leg. The athlete must be taught to let the right arm remain forward as he moves to the right foot, and then bring the left arm together with the right. Both arms are synchronized with the lead leg.

THE TAKE-OFF:

The take-off is continuation of the plant. As the foot reaches to the toe, the drive leg brings to pass to the take-off leg, with the knee driving upward. The ankle of the take-off leg must fully extend or planter flex. The lead knee must be driven away from the bar (for rotation) to the opposite standard and rise to at least waist height for full power development. The lower part of the lead leg must be perpendicular to the ground. The athlete should attempt to drive the knee to the height of the bar.

THE FLIGHT:

The flight portion of the jump is separate from the take-off. In this the jumper can gain height and set up conditions for bar clearance. Once the jumper has left the ground and has driven the lead-knee properly and kept the knee up, he will find the back to the bar in a position to be arched. The key to arch over the bar is the position of the head and the leg. If the jumper drops the head back, the body will arch and the hips will rise in an effort to clear the bar. In nutshell, the major features of the flight are:

- The take-off drive is maintained, i.e. the athlete "holds the vertical" after leaving the ground with the free knee and thigh held high.
- The long shape is achieved with arms and head held in the line of the body. The head should be fixed in the position by looking along the bar throughout the jump.
- For bar clearance, the heels are tucked up beneath the body with the hips splayed and knees apart. This results in the hips and thighs being held up.
- After the hips clear the bar the legs straighten, and the chin is tucked into the chest to assist to the lift of the legs away from the bar.

THE LANDING:

As the bar is cleared, the jumper flips the feet and the lower legs upwards at the knees and drops the hips to a sitting position. While descending toward the landing pad, the jumper moves the arms out to a lateral and slightly forward position. The chin is kept forward and down on the neck. Head is held high to assist landing on shoulders.

PRELIMINARY TAKE-OFF DRILLS:

Take-off is certainly difficult but it can be learnt through double foot take-off drill(s) and standing flop. In the former situation, the athlete stands with his back to the bar (which is set at hip level) about 30cm from it. Both knees are bent and the athlete springs up and over the bar landing on his shoulder. The following points should be emphasized in double foot take-off drills:

- All movements must be quick.
- There must be a great activity of the lower limbs. The body must be driven up the legs and not pulled over the bar by the arms or head.
- The initial lift is vertical, with minimum upper body towards the bar.
- The head is held fixed by looking along the bar towards the upright.

After sufficient practice, a standing flop is introduced by turning the athlete so that he faces the bar as he prepares to jump. The bar is set at hip level and the jumper stands at angle of 15 degree to it. The athlete bends both legs and jumps upward while simultaneously rotating along his vertical axis so that the clearance and landing can be affected on the back.

The same points of emphasis as in the back over are used in practicing the one stride flop, having the following characteristics:

- Short fast stride with fast knee drive
- Head fixed by looking down the bar
- Clearance assisted by head tuck

The complete action-sequence from run-up to landing is depicted in figure:

TRIPLE JUMP

Triple jump is a whole-action event (a single triple jump) and not three jumps – hop, step and jump – as earlier believed. It carries a sort of particular fascination for most people and thrill especially for younger boys because it underscores speed, straight, balance, technique, explosive jumping ability, rhythm, grace, kinetic awareness, patience and concentration as necessary components that versatile triple jumpers must possess.

TECHNIQUE:

The triple jump technique carries the following important elements:

THE APPROACH:

To have the better take-off, the athlete divides the runway into equal thirds from slow to fast to faster. The jumper should leave the broad at the highest speed that they can maintain through the contact point that that second phases.

High knee action helps prevent over-striding and also tends to keep the upper body in an exact posture. A good is "chest high, head high, and eye focus high".

For better jump use three check marks – a starting mark, another to mark the second or third time the plant foot hits, and another to mark the plant foot contact point between 38 and 45 feet from the take-off board.

TAKE OFF:

(Hop, first jump): The jumper should not lower his centre of gravity by flexing a leg on this step. Unlike in the longer jump, the goal in the triple jump is to maintain horizontal velocity. The athlete should focus eyes on the spot well past the board and a bit higher than the eye-level. The jumper must make a conscious effort to time pushing off from the ball of the take-off foot in synchronization with driving the knee of the free leg forward. The take-off foot should make contact with the board slightly in front of the hips. The shoulder should remain level through the take-off. Single or double arm combines with the knees drive at take-off to generate impulse that propels the take-off.

(Step, second jump): the upper body should be learning ahead of the hips to help maintain forward movements. The free leg should powerfully drive up to a 90degree position. The take-off leg will become the trail leg going into the next phase. A double0-arm action should be used at the take-off of the second phase. The jumping should first make contact with the heel of the foot, followed by an immediate rolling to a mid fort stance. The landing foot must be ahead of the hips at contact. The upper body should be relatively straight. Once the foot makes contact, the trail leg begins driving forward from its original position of being parallel to the ground position the arm and leg motion combine to aid forward movement, but they also create a greater force application through the take-off foot in the next phase.

(Jump, third jump): The body position at take-off for the same as that the previous phase. The arm momentum and the blocking motion contribute greatly to creating more ground force reaction and height. The knee must be forcefully driven up to at least at 90degreeat the hip. The jumper must continue to look forward once in the air, the jumper must keep the eyes forward and the chin up.

After take-off the athlete can go for arching back in air or holding the position as long as possible when he attains peak height. The leg is bent to bring them through to prepare to land. The jumper must make every effort to hold this position until the first contact with the sand.

THE LANDING:

At contact, the knees bent to help absorb the shock associated with landing. The arms should be in an extended position, moving backwards and the hands should be next to the buttocks at first contact. The athlete should avoid falling back. For this purpose, he can either use straight ahead method or slide-out method.

The complete action-sequence for the hop, step, and jump run as depicted in figures:

POLE VAULT

The pole vault is perhaps the most complex one-unified-and-undividable action event in track and field. It encompasses many of the skills of sprinters, jumpers and throwers.

TECHNIQUE:

The introduction on new, highly elastic poles has revolutionized the technique of vaulting as well as methods of training for it. Apart from the grip at the pole , the pole vault technique constitutes such elements as approach, pole carry & plant, take off, swing & rock, pull, turn and released.

APPROACH:

The length of the approach run varies with the individual, but it usually ranges from 100 to 150 feet. The approach run must be consistent. It should be made with maximum controllable speed, with the body in erect position reflecting good sprint mechanics.

CHECK MARKS:

Most pole vault athletes use 18-21 strides and three check marks. The first check marks are as the beginning stride. The second check mark is the coach's mark, 40 to 54 feet (6stride) away from the take-off. And the third check mark is the take-off.

POLE CARRY:

The pole should be carried in a position near the hip, with the back arm bent, and the front and backhand approximately the same distance from the hip. The distance between the varies with the individual, ranging from 18-36 inches. The planting end of the pole should initially be carried higher than the head and slightly to the left of the centre of line of the running for a right-hander. The vaulted should drop the pole gradually as he reaches the plant, controlling it until it hits the back of the box. The pole should never stop parallel to the ground during the drop. After the approach, the plant is the most important phase of the vault. The plant is initiated three to three-and-a-half stride out. In the beginning of the plant, the vaulted moves the pole with a wrist curl press-to-overhead action, placing the right arm as high as possible above and directly over the toe of the take-off foot.

There must be a smooth transition between the heads and arms to position the pole for the plant, the right arm then drives forward and upward in front of the head, while arms acts as a guide to direct the pole into the box.

The shoulder is kept square to the box at the plant. The key to a good vault is a high early, aggressive plant.

TAKE OFF:

For a good take off the following basic elements are required:

- The pole should be directly over the take-off foot.

- The right arm should be as high as possible.
- The lead knees have a quick, hard drive in leaving the ground, driving forward and upward.
- The left hand should keep the pole away from the body, but should be clasping a point to a right angle.
- The left leg should be completely extended, and as it is pulled through it should catch up with the right leg. The straight left leg enables the hip to lift.

SWING AND ROCK- BACK:

The swing transfers horizontal speed into vertical speed. During this period, the left leg begins to catch up with the right. This catching up process continues into the rock back position.

The rock-back phase maintains the momentum that was attained in the approach, plant and take-off. the right arm should be completely straight, with the left arm collapsing almost to a right angle, aligned with the pole, while still keeping the pole away from the body.

PULL, TURN, RELEASE:

The pull and turn begin when the pole is almost straight. They are almost simultaneous because the turn is started by the pull. This phase should be delayed as long as possible to achieve maximum vertical lift from the pole as it comes out of the bend. The vaulter is in an upward direction, not outward. The pull-and-turn is a quick, powerful movement with the vaulter finally extending his arm straight down the pole.

In releasing the vaulted gets off the pole and up and away from the bar, then he lands in the pit. A premature release could incomplete extension of the pole.

The distance running classifications are based on the primary energy source used during the event.

1. Short distance 800M
2. Middle distance 1500M
3. Long distance ....500M and 10000M

The goal of running mechanics is to achieve balanced movement of the body parts during running. Inefficient motion wastes energy.

- The torso is erect. There is very little forward lean, exert during acceleration. The athlete must run tall, with the hips forward.
- The foot should touchdown directly under the torso. The position of the foot as it touches down varies widely among runners.
- The legs move through among runners.
- The legs move through drive, recovery and support phases. Distance runners use less knee lift and recovery-leg kick then sprinters.
- The arms are used for balance and to transfer momentum, as in acceleration or a hill. The arms are carried at above at 90degree angle, swinging freely from the shoulders. They should not cross the middle of the body. The aggressiveness of arms moment is directly related to speed. The hands are cupped or curled comfortably, palms facing inward toward the middle of the body.
- The position of the head should be relatively level. The runner should look about 20m to30m ahead. Some runners look just below the horizon they are running. The base of the neck and shoulder should be relaxed also.

Following are some definitions associated with the scientific principals which affect the performance-

1. **Newton's Laws:**
   a) **Newton's First Law of motion.**
   b) **Newton's 2nd Law of Motion.**
   c) **Newton's 3rd Law of Motion.**
2. **Centripetal Force**
3. **Centrifugal Force**
4. **Parabola**
5. **Projectile**
6. **Head Wind**
7. **Tail Wind**
8. **Centre of Gravity**
9. **Line of Gravity**
10. **Angle of Release**

Newton's First Law

Newton's first law is called the Law of Inertia because it outlines a key property of matter related to motion. Newton stated that all objects have the inherent property to resist a change in their state of motion. His first law is usually stated something like this: objects tend to stay at rest or in uniform motion unless acted upon by an unbalanced force. In simple words, any object remains to be in state of rest or uniform motion until an external force is not applied on that body. It is always used in events like, crouch stars, in the starting of throwing and jumping events etc.

Newton's Second Law: Newton's second law is arguably the most important law of motion because it shows how the forces that create motion (kinetics) are linked to the motion (kinematics). The second law is called the Law of Momentum or Law of Acceleration, depending on how the mathematics is written. The most common approach is the famous F = ma.

Newton's Third Law: - Newton's third law of motion is called the Law of Reaction, because it is most often translated as: for every action there is an equal and opposite reaction. For every force exerted, there is an equal and opposite force being exerted. Lets take an example of an athlete who is going to take the start for short race, 100m. On the command of the starter, "On Your Mark", Set, and Gun Fire, the athlete pushes the starting block and similarly he receives the push from the block. The amount of force he exerted on the block, he is going to experience the same amount of push.

Contact Forces (Friction): The linear kinetics of the interaction of two objects in contact is also analyzed by resolving the forces into right-angle components. These components use a local frame of reference like the two-dimensional muscle angle of pull above, because using horizontal and vertical components are not always convenient.

Principal of Spin

The Principle of Spin is related to using the spin on a projectile to obtain an advantageous trajectory or bounce. Kinesiology professionals can use the principle of spin to understand the most successful techniques in many activities.

Centripetal Force and centrifugal force:-

When a body or an object revolves in a circular path, there are two important forces which act on the body to make the body move in the circular path. Centripetal Force is the force which attracts the body towards the center and the Centrifugal Force repels it outwards. Both of these forces are equal in amount. If any of the forces increases by a small bit, the object surely is going to break the circular path.

Projectile:

A projectile is an object thrown into space by the exertion of a force. Although any object in motion through space (for example a thrown hammer may be called a projectile, the term more commonly refers to a ranged weapon.)

Tail Wind and Head wind:

A tail wind is a wind that blows in the direction of travel of an object, while a headwind blows against the direction of travel. A Tailwind increases the object's speed and reduces the time required to reach its destination, while a headwind has the opposite effect.

Centre of Gravity:

The centre of gravity of an object is the point at which weight is evenly dispersed and all sides are in balance. A Human's center of gravity can change as he takes on different positions, but in many other objects, it's a fixed location.

Line of Gravity:

Line of gravity is an imaginary vertical line from the centre of gravity to the ground or surface the object or a person is on. The closer the line of gravity is to the center of the base of the support, the better balanced a person is in this position.

Angle of Release:

For an object released at ground level, for any given release velocity, the maximum distance is achieved using an angle of approximately 45 degrees, and for the hammer throw it is 43-44 degrees.